Rose's Dilemma

A Play

by Neil Simon

A SAMUEL FRENCH ACTING EDITION

SAMUEL FRENCH

FOUNDED 1830

New York Hollywood London Toronto

SAMUELFRENCH.COM

ISBN   978-0-573-60262-7   Printed   in   U.S.A.   #170

IMPORTANT BILLING AND CREDIT REQUIREMENTS

All producers of ROSE'S DILEMMA *must* give credit to the Author of the Play in all programs distributed in connection with performances of the Play and in all instances in which the title of the Play appears for purposes of advertising, publicizing or otherwise exploiting the Play and/or a production. The name of the Author *must* appear on a separate line on which no other name appears, immediately following the title, and *must* appear in size of type not less than fifty percent the size of the title type.

MANHATTAN THEATRE CLUB
CITY CENTER STAGE I

Artistic Director
Lynne Meadow

Executive Producer
Barry Grove

Presents

Rose's Dilemma

by

Neil Simon

with

David Aaron Baker

Geneva Carr

John Cullum

Patricia Hodges

Set Design
Thomas Lynch

Costume Design
William Ivey Long

Lighting Design
Pat Collins

Sound Design
Bruce Ellman

Wig Design
Paul Huntley

Production Stage Manager
Robert Witherow

Directed by

Lynne Meadow

Casting
**Nancy Piccione/David Caparelliotis
Jay Binder**

Press Representative
Boneau/Bryan-Brown

Production Manager/
Director of Capital Projects
Michael R. Moody

Director of Development
Andrew D. Hamingson

Director of Marketing
Debra A. Waxman

General Manager
Harold Wolpert

Director of Artistic Development
Paige Evans

Rose and Walsh, an earlier version of this play, was originally produced by the Geffen Playhouse.

ACT I

Scene 1

(THE BEACH HOUSE.
WALSH and ROSE on the patio—ARLENE at the table inside...
WALSH walks away and ROSE goes inside.)

ARLENE. What were you doing outside?

ROSE. Nothing. Just looking at the moon...Where were we?

ARLENE. Alright...Flowers.

ROSE. What about flowers?

ARLENE. You've got to cut down on flowers, Rose. You've got the botanical gardens growing in here.

ROSE. I need my flowers. They sweeten my life.

ARLENE. And they're destroying your bank account. Get artificial flowers. They don't die.

ROSE. And they don't smell either. I need aroma. A room without flowers is like a house without air. I can't write unless I can breathe. Especially without a man in my life...

ARLENE. What's a man got to do with it?

ROSE. A woman has to smell *some*thing...Especially at my age... Did you ever really smell a strong interesting man?...If they could bottle that, there'd be no lonely women in the world.

ARLENE. I've dated a few who wore the wrong cologne. The date was over before I opened the door.

ROSE. Exactly...Walsh never wore the wrong cologne. His body just emitted the essence of who he was...The smell of strength...The odor of intelligence...The aroma of sexuality.

ARLENE. I'll take a dozen...Now can we continue trying to save

5

you from bankruptcy and disaster?

ROSE. Why? Did you ever smell money? Hard cash? It has the odor of a thousand greasy fingers on it...You don't know who touched it, where it's been, and what diseased thing it slept with.

ARLENE. Rose...It's a quarter to one in the morning...We've been at this all night and we still haven't cut out a nickel from your budget... Your bills keep mounting, your debts increasing...and *still* you made fresh lobster for dinner.

ROSE. I didn't notice you turning down any claws.

ARLENE. You're a great cook, Rose. But a tuna salad would be just as filling and one tenth the price.

ROSE. Rub your tongue in the cracks of your teeth. So good, that if you didn't brush your teeth, there's enough leftovers in there for tomorrow.

ARLENE. You can't pay your bills with what's left in the cracks of your teeth. You haven't sold or written a book or a short story or an idea on a napkin for over five years.

ROSE. Since Walsh died...I think I only wrote to hear what he thought of it.

ARLENE. Get rid of the flowers, cut out the lobsters or write birthday cards for Hallmark before you go bust, Rose.

ROSE. You need more sensuality in your life, Arlene...Have you had any lately?

ARLENE. Not with lobster in the cracks of my teeth.

ROSE. Alright....Don't say anymore...Let me think.

(She rests her head on the back of the chair, closes her eyes.)

ARLENE. *(Looks around the room.)* You bought six new books this month and you haven't read one of them...You have to stop deliveries to the house, Rose.

ROSE. *(Softly, with eyes closed.)* I love deliveries......
ARLENE. Rose...Rose...Can you hear me?

(But ROSE seems to be somewhere else...From somewhere in the room, a man appears, in his sixties, wearing an old white bath-

robe, pajamas and slippers. This is the ghost of WALSH.)

WALSH. She's right, Rose...How many photos do you have of me around the house?...Two dollars worth of film wrapped in three thousand dollars of silver frames from Tiffany's...You don't need it and I'm not worth it.

ROSE. You are to me.

ARLENE. I am to you what?

ROSE. *(Her eyes open.)* Hmm?...Oh...I just closed my eyes for a second...Sorry.

ARLENE. You were talking to him again, weren't you?...Another midnight chat with Walsh McLaren?

ROSE. Walsh is gone...No one can talk to him.

ARLENE. I think you spend more time in that world than in this one.

ROSE. I don't encourage it. I don't ask him to come. He pops in on his own.

ARLENE. You must have *some*thing to do with it.

ROSE. Well, I'm sitting here, he says something to me, I can't be impolite, can I?

WALSH. *(Appears again.)* Sorry, Rose. You call me. I can't get here without you thinking of me. I can't meet you in a hotel unless you book the room.

ROSE. *(To ARLENE.)* It only happens now and then. I'm trying to cut down.

ARLENE. What are you looking at?

ROSE. I miss him. Is that alright to say?

ARLENE. I miss my dead father too but I don't talk to him every night...Let it go, Rose. It's five years now.

ROSE. Five years, fifty years. What's that got to do with it?

ARLENE. I have an analyst who told me that half the widows in the world still speak to their dead spouses.

ROSE. No wonder I have so much trouble getting through to Walsh.

ARLENE. She knows one woman who's been talking to her dead husband for 41 years...and now she wants a divorce.

ROSE. You don't find that inspiring?

ARLENE. I'm not even married, Rose. I'm not looking for an after life experience.

ROSE. Why not? You take what life has left to give you.

ARLENE. Don't make up phrases, Rose. There's no such saying.

ROSE. Yes, there is. I said it. I wrote it. I'm Rose Steiner. I'm a famous writer.

ARLENE. Then don't talk to him at night. Write a book about it. "Rose and Walsh"...It would bring some money into the house.

ROSE. God, no...He'd come back from the grave and rip the brains out of my typewriter.

ARLENE. *(Closes book.)* It's late, Rose...I need at least an hour and a half of sleep a night...I'm going to bed...Don't buy any flowers tonight...They're beginning to creep up into my bedroom.... *(Gathers her papers together.)* Are you coming up?

ROSE. In a while...I always love sitting in this room.

ARLENE. You're going to talk to him again, aren't you?

ROSE. No, I promise I won't...We're both too tired.

ARLENE. Because if you do, I'll run the shower.

(She goes off as WALSH comes out from somewhere else.)

WALSH. *(Watches ARLENE leave, then turns to ROSE, and snaps his fingers.)* Up up up, Rose. Don't waste these precious moments...What were we talking about?

ROSE. When?

WALSH. Last week, last month, five years ago...You remember those things, I don't.

ROSE. Five years ago you were alive, Walsh. Do you remember being alive?

WALSH. Yes. The food tasted better then...Hell, I remember when I was twenty two...I had a full head of thick hair that stood straight up like an African plant and I wore a Dapper Dan grey tweed suit that wouldn't wrinkle if I was in a flood.

ROSE. *(This wakes her.)* YES!...I love when you spit out the dialogue like fireworks.

WALSH. Jesus, we were a hot couple...You weren't a kid, Rose, but you were the first dame I spotted at that bar.

ROSE. I reeled you in like a tiger shark...kicking and fighting for your life.

WALSH. "Pull me in, baby," I yelled...Hey! Whose apartment was it that we almost destroyed that night?

ROSE. My husband's...Well, we weren't married then...Cute little bald guy who knew how to hold on to a job...something that couldn't have occurred to you...but I needed someone like you to break the stallion in me.

WALSH. Hell, you weren't a stallion...You were the lead buffalo in a Texas stampede.

(She throws her head back and laughs.)

ROSE. Damn right I was...wasn't I?

WALSH. Hey! How'd we end up in Mexico that night?

ROSE. We stole a car and headed south looking for cheaper gas.

WALSH. *(Laughs.)* Ay yi yi Dolores.....We got thrown into a truckful of avocados and peanut shells...Ended up in a San Diego bar eating raw crabs and catfish.

ROSE. What about that brawl? You knocked out a priest wearing a sombrero.

WALSH. Police chased us back across the Mexican border and we ended up in a town with nothing but prisons.

ROSE. We had separate cells but we still managed to have the best night of love making down Mehico way...God damn, that was fun.

WALSH. We made love from separate cells?

ROSE. Damn right.

WALSH. I don't remember that.

ROSE. Sure you do. The mayor was throwing flowers and tortillas at us.

WALSH. That never happened.

ROSE. Well, let's leave it in anyway. They're just memories, let's throw it in the pot.

*(They laugh as ARLENE makes an appearance in robe and slippers...
She walks softly with her head down.)*

ARLENE. Sorry...Excuse me...Just getting a cup of tea.

(She goes into the kitchen.)

ROSE. *(To WALSH.)* We should have gone upstairs.

WALSH. Why? She can't see us anyway.

ROSE. Well, not you. Just me...But she can hear us.

WALSH. She can?

ROSE. Well, not you. Just me.

WALSH. Talking to yourself?

ROSE. Well, just me. Not you....Where've you been? I've been waiting for you all night.

WALSH. Well, truth is, something's come up, Rose...I didn't know how you'd react.....I've been pounding this beat for a long time, babe.

ROSE. Oh, don't babe me. They don't say babe anymore...You sound like a caricature of yourself that fell off the wall at Sardi's.

WALSH. I was never on the wall at Sardi's. The last thing I'd want to do is watch people who go to musicals eating dinner. *(Points to sofa.)* May I sit?

ROSE. Men don't ask if they can sit anymore...They just sit...You have to keep up with things, Walsh.

WALSH. I need some time off, Rose. It's been a lot of years now and I'm getting lonely for my crowd...

ROSE. Like who? Scott and Zelda? Marcel Proust?

WALSH. They're better off than I am, Rose. They're in the hereafter. I'm in the "still up and running around."

ROSE. I knew this was coming. I always hated the sight of your packed suitcase standing in the hall.

WALSH. Be honest, Rose. Sometimes it was you who packed the suitcase and threw it in the hallway.

ROSE. I didn't see any point waiting for the inevitable.

WALSH. Well, that's true. A man usually makes too many promises in bed. Not that I ever intended to keep any of them...Hell, I always had to pay for my passion one way or another.

ROSE. A twenty dollar bill on the night table would have had more integrity.

WALSH. You think too much of me, Rose. I rarely had the integrity *or* the twenty dollar bill.

(ARLENE comes out of the kitchen holding a cup of tea, her head is down.)

ARLENE. Sorry...Excuse me.

(She is off.)

WALSH. We've got to talk, Rose.

ROSE. Let's go up to the bedroom before she comes down looking for a lobster sandwich...I'll grab some champagne, we'll turn on a little retro music.

WALSH. There isn't much time for that, Rose.

ROSE. We have time for everything.... *(He looks to see if ARLENE is there. She lowers her voice.)* You don't have a bad heart anymore. You've got a back like a young man now...Please come to my room, Walsh...I hate it when we make love and you're still down here.

WALSH. Things are not the same now...Time diminishes everything...Thanks to your vivid imagination, it worked for us for years... but the light is fading, Rose. Everything comes harder for us now.

ROSE. What I want, I can still make happen.

WALSH. How many times do you have to call for me to come in from the beach? The signals get weaker, kid...But I come night after night because I make the effort...*My* effort...But my effort and your imagination don't last forever...You mean too much to me to see you losing your independence...If I have to leave, I won't do it without paying you back for more love and affection that any human being, man or woman, ever gave me and never once asked me to settle up the tab.

ROSE. That's from one of my plays. I wrote that speech.

WALSH. You write *every* speech. Every word I say, every thought is yours. That's why we've gotten along so well after all these years. I'm trying to help you, dammit. Can't you see that?

ROSE. By turning me down? By threatening to leave? This is *my* dream, Walsh, not yours. And in my dream I don't diminish. I'm at the apex of my prime, kiddo...I lectured at twelve universities last year and some of the standing ovations I got are still standing.

WALSH. I'm not questioning the eternal quickness of your mind, Rose. Just the inability of it to bring a buck in the house.

ROSE. I'm not interested in a buck...A *young* buck, yes...

WALSH. Did I tell you it's my birthday in two weeks? I'll be 65...

ROSE. I know.

WALSH. In my day, it was time to retire...My time is over here. The point is, Rose, I'm still going, whether you imagined these years or not. Neither of us can stop the clock from ticking...You can't see the morning newspaper, can you.

ROSE. Nor do I want to. You want to know why I don't wear my glasses anymore...Because you're not all that attractive at 20-20...Two more weeks, is that all I've got...My God, I'll have my nights free. You'd like that, wouldn't you, Walshy?

WALSH. You know how that is, Rose. Some things, like writing or dying, are best done alone.

ROSE. And quite frankly, sex with a dead man isn't *half* as good as I was led to believe.

WALSH. Still, I don't want to leave you broke and impoverished, Rose...How much money have you got?

ROSE. We have plenty. We had three lobsters for dinner.

WALSH. None of it covers what you spend to redecorate this house every year. You've got four closets filled with four wardrobes and you still keep wearing that same black Chanel suit they've been waiting for at the Smithsonian.

ROSE. Never judge a woman by what she wears. It's what she buys that counts.

WALSH. You're going into bankruptcy, kid. How are you going to live? How will you pay your bills?

ROSE. I'll stoop to writing major motion pictures.

WALSH. I know a better way.

ROSE. I am not selling your love letters. You wrote them while you were drunk and I had to rewrite everything.

WALSH. I know where you can lay your hands on a basketful of cash. There's a hot book floating around just begging to be published.

ROSE. Tell them you're not 65. You lied about your age.... What's their rush, dammit! I need you more than they do.

WALSH. The book is "Mexican Standoff"... An uncompleted novel.

ROSE. Whose uncompleted novel?

WALSH. Mine...I had thirty, maybe forty more pages to go when I suddenly had that heart attack...at the luncheon you gave on the patio...Do you remember?

ROSE. Of course I remember. I served striped bass.

WALSH. No. About the heart attack. I tried telling you at the luncheon. I whispered, "Get an ambulance," but you thought I was talking about the fish.

ROSE. Why do you make me go back to that, Walsh?....It was the worst day of my life.

WALSH. I wanted to give you the book but I couldn't move...It's in the cabinet, over there, under the window. I was going to tell you about it after the luncheon...except I couldn't speak.

ROSE. Your face turned white and your hands were cold...I knew it was over then, Walsh, and somehow I wanted to go with you.

WALSH. The book is still in there, Rose. I kept it there for you.

ROSE. I don't want your unfinished book, Walsh. That should go to a college or the Library of Congress.

WALSH. They don't need money. You do.

ROSE. Money is easy to get. Literature is impossible. Give it to the world, Walsh, not me.

WALSH. Then why did you make me think of it just now?

ROSE. I didn't. I haven't thought of it in years.

WALSH. Really? You must have found the book in there once but you would never tell me. Never even read it....And now that I'm going—

ROSE. Again.

WALSH. For the last time, you reminded me of the book.

ROSE. Not for myself, Walsh, I swear.

WALSH. You don't have to swear. You want what I wrote, and you saved it. I want it to fulfill the rest of your life...Come on, Rose. Open the cabinet. Let's take a look at it.

ROSE. Do it yourself. It's not my book.

WALSH. Rose, you know I can't open doors, I can't hold inanimate objects. Come on! Kneel down. Get on your knees.

ROSE. You haven't asked me to do that in a long time.

(Slowly, she gets down on one knee.)

WALSH. Now pull the cabinet open. *(She pulls and the cabinet opens.)* Alright, what do you see in there?

ROSE. Dust I've been saving for years.

WALSH. *(Leans over.) Under* the dust. I can see it from here. Grab the package, Rose.

(She pulls out a paper covered book.)

ROSE. Help me up.

WALSH. You know I can't do that.

ROSE. *(Holds cabinet, pulls herself up.)* I always wondered how those elderly Catholic women get up after mass.

WALSH. That's the book, Rosie...Take off the paper.

ROSE. That's my old Christmas wrapping.

WALSH. And your present is in there... *(She tears it off.)* Open to the first page.

(She opens it, looks at it.)

ROSE. "MEXICAN STANDOFF"...by Walsh McLaren... *(She weighs it in her hand.)* Yeah. Feels about 40 pages light..... How did you remember it was in here after all these years?

WALSH. Someone's been keeping me alive, Kid.

ROSE. Damn right.....This doesn't belong to me, Walsh. Give it to your ex-wife....What was her name? I forget.

WALSH. Tell me.

ROSE. Frieda.

WALSH. That's right. Frieda.

ROSE. And what would I do with an unfinished book?

WALSH. Finish it.

ROSE. With you?

WALSH. Me? No...I've been interred, Rose...I can't create, recreate or procreate....You're going to do it.

ROSE. *Me*?.....I can't even see the typewriter these days.

WALSH. I've got someone to see it for you. See that paperback..."Rest in Pieces"..by Gavin Clancy...I found it in my bathrobe pocket. I don't know who put it there...This Clancy kid—doesn't know the first thing about structure or character but he can write, Rosey....He can twirl a sentence in the air like a ring of smoke... Published by Delacorte...Call them up, find out where this kid is and get him over...Between him, you and me, we can turn out the best piece of mystery fiction in the last thirty years.

ROSE. But you're going away, Walsh...

WALSH. You know I wouldn't turn down an opportunity like this.

ROSE. But you've only got two weeks left.

WALSH. We'll work night and day...Downstairs and upstairs.

ROSE. No...I can't do it...I can't write like you and neither can some cheap paperback scribbler...if it's not your book, it's a fraud, Walsh, which is the one thing in the world you never were.

WALSH. I'll be in there with you pitching, Kid...I'll watch the prose, you watch the style and let the scribbler watch the sex. Trust me, Rosie, I know what I'm doing.

ROSE. Do you?...I'm the one who needs watching...I knew that book was in there for years...I knew it wasn't any good without you... or me to help...I thought of it, Walsh...I hoped for it...Damn it, I *dreamed* of it....Don't you understand what I've done?

WALSH. You think I didn't know that?....You think I don't know how your mind works after all these years dead *and* alive?....I owe you all the joy in my life, Rose, and I'm not going to let that book collect dust in the cabinet...Geez, it feels good to be back in the saddle again...Meet me up in your room, Rosie....After five years, it's time I took off this bathrobe...and got back to writing.

(He goes off. ROSE looks up to where her room is with a big smile.)

ROSE. Arlene???...I'm coming up to bed...Turn on your shower.

(Go to black.)

Scene 2

(The next morning, bright and shiny. ARLENE sits at the breakfast table, just finishing up a telephone call.)

ARLENE. *(Into phone.)* ...Oh, she called *you* this morning...at nine o'clock...She rarely does that...Okay...Gavin Clancy... Quogue...631-472-8639...Got it...I certainly will...Well, thank you very much, Mr. Delacorte....She'll be very pleased to hear that....

(She hangs up as ROSE comes down the stairs in a classy robe.)

ROSE. I'd be pleased to hear what?
ARLENE. That Mr. Delacorte is a big fan...You look very chipper this morning.
ROSE. I got lucky in bed. *(Pours herself coffee.)* Who is Mr. Delacorte?
ARLENE. A publisher...He said you called him at nine a.m. this morning.
ROSE. Oh, was that me?...I was *urged* to do it.
ARLENE. He said Mr. Clancy is in Quogue and would be thrilled to see you...he left Clancy's number.

ROSE. Quogue?....That's only a short distance from here...Tell me again what Mr. Clancy does.

ARLENE. He wrote "Rest in Pieces"...He said you'd know.

ROSE. I'd be the only one... *(She looks in mirror.)* God, what a night...Do I look younger?

ARLENE. Younger than what?

ROSE. Younger than springtime.

ARLENE. Yes, you do. A little like early April...I'm glad you slept well. I closed my door and took a sleeping pill when I heard you cry out, "oh, yes. Yes, yes" ....I've got to draw the line someplace...

ROSE. Good. Then you didn't hear the rest of the night. Walsh found the last book he wrote. "Mexican Standoff."

ARLENE. I never heard of it.

ROSE. He never finished it. He died at the luncheon.

ARLENE. I'm sorry I didn't get to read it.

ROSE. Every writer dies with an unfinished novel. It's some sort of affectation...He wants to get it finished and leave me the royalties... I'd be rich as Croesus.

ARLENE. It sounds like a busy night. How is he going to finish it?

ROSE. Well, there are still 40 pages to finish. He can't do it and I certainly won't try. He has however, picked a ghost writer... I can't believe I said that.

ARLENE. Would that be Mr. Clancy?

ROSE. A paperback author he found in his bathrobe pocket. Gavin Clancy from Delacorte.

ARLENE. How fortunate for you and Walsh.

ROSE. Arlene, my bedroom love stories are really self-imposed torture sessions. It doesn't mean our love was that great. It means my need is so desperate. I'm a prisoner of my own romanticism, sitting here night after night, waiting to go up to my bedroom and simulate simulated sex.

ARLENE. If you don't believe it's real, why are you so afraid of losing him?

ROSE. Because I'm afraid I won't make it through the rest of my life alone...Having Walsh here is like putting up signs all over the walls. "Think" over my typewriter…"Stop" over the liquor cabinet. … "Sleep" over my bed… "Truth" over my conscience.

ARLENE. The only signs men put up in my life were "goodbye" and "I'm borrowing your car." How would you feel if you never saw him again?

ROSE. It hasn't happened as yet….not without me putting up a helluva fight.

ARLENE. Why do you hold on so much, Rose?

ROSE. He keeps me going. He keeps me on my toes and reminds me of what I'm supposed to do with my life. I still feel young around him. Sometimes I can almost feel his hands touching me, although he's smart enough never to try. The game has its rules and I have to abide by them….Still, we have fun together and the most wonderful, exasperating arguments…and miraculously still make love up there.

ARLENE. How?

ROSE. Well, it takes enormous concentration and a *huge* personal investment. His afterlife is my best creation and if keeping him means losing my sanity, I would consider it a fair exchange…

ARLENE. The truth Rose? I'm envious of what you have.

ROSE. Arlene…have you fallen in love with Walsh?

ARLENE. If I have, you have no one to blame but yourself.

ROSE. That bastard. I knew I couldn't trust him.

ARLENE. Come on, Rose. It isn't exactly adultery.

ROSE. He'll find a way. Do you think this book is Walsh's idea or my own mercenary invention?

ARLENE. Maybe a little of both. Another sign on the wall. "Survive." Forget the book. Let's kick Walsh out of the house and let's both start a new life.

ROSE. Not yet. Give me Clancy's number. *(ARLENE gives her the* N.Y. Times, *points to it. ROSE looks at it and dials.)* Quogue? That's too convenient. Never trust a dead man you're living with. What do I say to him? "Walsh McLaren asked me to call you?…Yes, I know he's dead, but I've been busy lately." *(She waits.)* Five rings…..he sleeps too late to be any good. *(Into phone.)* Hello…Is this Gavin Clancy?…This is Rose Steiner….Yes. The writer….No. It's not a gag….I don't gag in the morning…I got your number from

Delacorte........That *is* your publisher, if I may ask?...Oh, that long ago.... *(To ARLENE.)* I think Walsh picked someone deader than he is. *(Back into phone.)* This may sound strange to you Mr. Clancy, as it does to me, but I have a business proposition for you...Well, I need some help on a book I'm writing and someone suggested you....Well, if you must know, it was Walsh McLaren...He read your book, "Rest in Pieces"...Yes, I know your book came out after he died.....maybe he received an advance copy..... *(To ARLENE, hand over the phone.)* He's laughing....Sounds like he's on drugs...

(WALSH enters from the side.)

WALSH. He's just nervous. He knows he's out of his league.

ROSE. *(To WALSH.)* Then why don't *you* talk to him?

ARLENE. Me? I spoke to Mr. Delacorte. I did my part.

WALSH. Tell him to come over. Have a cup of tea with him.

ROSE. He doesn't drink tea. He only takes stimulants with a needle.

ARLENE. *(Looks around.)* Oh, my God. Is Walsh in the room?

ROSE. *(To ARLENE.)* No, he's not in the room. He's in my head manipulating me. *(Into phone.)* Mr. Clancy, may I suggest we talk this out over tea?...*Tea*...Alright, beer will be fine.....Here at my place.

WALSH. Reel him in slowly ...Don't give him too much slack.

ROSE. *(Into phone.)* Can I put my assistant on? She'll give you directions...How's two o'clock?

WALSH. No. I'm with my analyst at two o'clock. Make it nine.

ROSE. *(Into phone.)* Or can you make it at nine?...Yes. In the evening.

WALSH. Eleven is better.

ROSE. Eleven is better. *(To WALSH.)* Why? What are you doing at nine?

WALSH. I meet with my stockbroker.

ROSE. *(To ARLENE.)* Talk to him.

ARLENE. Hello? Mr. Clancy? This is Arlene...I'm fine, thanks, and you?

WALSH. *(To ROSE.)* Don't let her get into a conversation with him. It takes up time.

(ROSE gestures to ARLENE to hurry it along.)

ARLENE. *(Into phone.)* Well, do you know where the Old Bridge road is?...In East Hampton...The Old Bridge Road.

WALSH. Send a cab for him.

ARLENE. *(To ROSE.)* Can he see me? Walsh, I mean.

ROSE. Yes. He thinks you're very attractive.

ARLENE. *(Back into phone.)* Mr. Clancy? Alright, forget the Old Bridge Road. Do you know where Duck Lane is?...That's right. Just past the Old Bridge Road.

ROSE. If he can't think, how can be write?

ARLENE. Number 206...

WALSH. Ask him what kind of beer he likes.

ROSE. Ask him what kind of beer he likes.

ARLENE. *(Into phone.)* He said Heineken.

WALSH. What about a corned beef sandwich?

ROSE. How about a lobster salad?

ARLENE. There isn't any. You ate it last night.

WALSH. You finished the lobster salad?

ROSE. I was hungry!

(ROSE grabs the phone from ARLENE.)

ARLENE. No, it's your first left; just after the Old Bridge Road...

ROSE. The Old Bridge Road you moron! In North America!

(Black out.)

Scene 3

About 11PM. ROSE paces, wearing a white woolen sweater with a drink in her hand. ARLENE sits, watching her.)

ARLENE. *(Looks at her watch.)* Five minutes to eleven. *(To ROSE.)* How long should I stay?

ROSE. Until Walsh shows up.

ARLENE. How will I know when he shows up?

ROSE. I get funnier....and more seductive... *(The doorbell rings.)* No. That's not Walsh...There's not enough of him left to ring a doorbell...Let the paperback writer in.

(ROSE crosses to the door to the beach.)

ARLENE. Where are you going?

ROSE. I want to make an entrance. Then I have the advantage.

ARLENE. *(Crosses to the beach door.)* What do I say to him?

ROSE. *(Exiting.)* Can I get you a Heineken?

(She is gone.
GAVIN CLANCY enters as ARLENE is half out the door. CLANCY knocks on the wooden wall. She turns and looks at him. He is wearing a rumpled sports jacket, open shirt, worn sneakers. His hair needs grooming and his face needs shaving yet there's something attractive about him. He's about Arlene's age.)

ARLENE. Oh. You let yourself in....I'm Arlene.

CLANCY. Yeah. You looked too young for Rose.

ARLENE. Please come in.... *(He looks around. Impressed.)* Did you have any trouble finding the house?

CLANCY. I don't think so. I'm five minutes early...I went past the Old Bridge Road.

ARLENE. Well, Miss Steiner just went out to...to...I'm not sure where she went out to——but she'll be right back....Can I get you a Heineken?

CLANCY. No, thanks. Just had one....She likes beer?

ARLENE. Not really. She had me go out and buy a case.

CLANCY. Oh? It's gonna be a long meeting...Do you know what this thing's about? This writing proposition?

ARLENE. Yes...Well, not really. She'll tell you.

CLANCY. You just give out directions here.

ARLENE. No. I'm a friend. Well, more than a friend...She's my writing mentor.

CLANCY. I'm a writer, too...already mentored.

ARLENE. Yes, she mentioned that...What do you do now if I may ask?

CLANCY. That's what she said... "If I may ask" ....I don't write those kinds of books. *(He looks at bookshelf.)* She write all of these?

ARLENE. Yes, she did.

CLANCY. So what does she want with some faded ex-writer who has one paperback on his shelf...if I had a shelf.

ARLENE. Well, I'm sure she'll tell you that.

CLANCY. Why not?...You're very polite...She mentor your manners too?

(ROSE walks in from outside.)

ROSE. Ah. You're on time, Mr. Clancy...You *are* Mr. Clancy? Well, you didn't have to dress.

CLANCY. So I guess this isn't a gag after all.

ROSE. If you thought it was a gag, why did you come, if I may ask?

(At that, he smiles at ARLENE.)

CLANCY. I could use the money. If I don't get the writing job, I could paint your house.

ROSE. My house never needs painting. I have a man from Sotheby's come out every winter and paint it with a very small brush.

CLANCY. Well, I could stay and prune your garden...or does Christie's do that?

ROSE. *(Looks at him.)* ... and I wondered why you gave up writing.

(She gives him a fake smile. WALSH comes out, looks CLANCY over.)

WALSH. Just what I pictured...Some slob who dresses down to

impress the natives that he's an artist.

CLANCY. *(To ROSE.)* So er...just the two of you live here?

ROSE. Why do you ask?

CLANCY. Well, the guy at the gas station said there used to be a fella here. An older guy. Another writer, I think.

ROSE. No. He was a Christmas tree tinseler.

WALSH. Don't challenge him, Rosey.

ARLENE. He's just trying to be friendly.

ROSE. Oh, Arlene. We're keeping you from bed. I won't stop you, if you insist.

ARLENE. Well, I have been up since dawn...Goodnight, Mr. Clancy...It was a pleasure meeting you.

CLANCY. Thanks for the directions...I'd have driven right into the Atlantic...belly up.

(She smiles and goes off.)

WALSH. *(To ROSE's ear.)* Let's lessen the tension in here, Rose. Make him feel comfortable...

ROSE. *(To CLANCY.)* If there's a chair in here that you like, Mr. Clancy, you can sit in it.

CLANCY. *(Doesn't sit.)* Look, I'll be honest with you...I don't know why you picked me and what you picked me for...I've seen a couple of your plays, read some of your books, you're uptown, I'm downtown. I don't think I fit in here but why don't we just get to it... what's up?

WALSH. *(To ROSE.)* He's nervous....He knows who you are and who he's *not*...Flatter him about his book.

ROSE. *(To CLANCY.)* I don't usually read books like yours.

CLANCY. Well, I don't really write them for people like you.

WALSH. *(To ROSE.)* No, no. *Flatter* him. Tell him you liked it, for Christ sakes.

ROSE. *(To CLANCY.)* So it's just the one book, is it?

CLANCY. Well, I was a one book man, Miss Steiner. You throw a stone, make a ripple in the water and two years later you sink to the bottom. I just ran out of stones, Ma'am.

ROSE. Pity that literature lost such a colorful character.

WALSH. *(To ROSE.)* What are you doing, Rose? You're losing him. Give him a beer. Get him a Heineken.

CLANCY. I got by. Wrote a few magazine articles, spent a year in a garage, I'm good with cars, worked on a freighter hauling oil to South America and a short stint as a private detective.

WALSH. *(Excited.)* A *private detective.* So was the guy in "Mexican Standoff".... Grab him, Rose. Tie him up, nail him to the floor.

ROSE. *(To CLANCY.)* And what if I gave you an idea that might start your engines up again? One that could make a resounding splash at Doubleday...Would you be interested?

WALSH. Of *course* he'd be interested. *(His face in CLANCY's.)* Tell her you'd be interested. *(To ROSE.)* He's interested. He's interested.

CLANCY. *(Not too enthusiastic.)* Yeah, I'd be interested.

WALSH. *(To ROSE.)* We got him! We got him! Make him an offer! Give him a deal!

ROSE. *(To WALSH, angrily.) Will you stop it!*

(ROSE makes a fist to WALSH.)

CLANCY. Did I say something wrong?

ROSE. *(Grabs her back.)* No, no I get back spasms....It's alright. *(Hands CLANCY the book.)* Here's the book I'm working on. Read it. Tell me what you think. I took off the title page so you wouldn't be intimidated by my name.

CLANCY. *(Takes it.)* Got ya. I don't know who wrote it, okay?... Give me a few days with it.

WALSH. NO!!! We don't have a few days. We only have two weeks.

ROSE. I *know* that.

CLANCY. Know what?

ROSE. I know that the publisher will be calling me. He must have the book in two weeks.

CLANCY. In two weeks? Why?

WALSH. So they can get the book out by Christmas.

ROSE. *(To CLANCY.)* So they can get the book out by Christmas.

CLANCY. Why? They already *have* too many books out at Christmas.

WALSH. *(Into CLANCY's face.)* It's a winter book, you Goddam idiot. I'm giving you a break just letting you read it.

ROSE. *(To CLANCY.)* It's what they call a winter book. Heavy enough to keep you warm and smart enough to keep you from going for a swim.

CLANCY. I don't get it but I like you, Miss Steiner. Sure. Count me in....Oh. If I do it, do I get a credit?

ROSE. Yes.

WALSH. No.

ROSE. Maybe.

CLANCY. Which is it?

ROSE. Isn't it enough you'll be well paid?

CLANCY. Yeah. It'll be enough....Will your friend be working with us?

WALSH. *Me?*

ROSE. Who?

CLANCY. Your assistant?

WALSH. Oh. He means the girl.

ROSE. Arlene. Yes, if you like.

CLANCY. It's nice to have someone around to sharpen the pencils....so when do I read it?

ROSE. Now. Tonight. In here. I'm going up to bed.

CLANCY. I read quickly. What do I do when I finish?

WALSH. Read it again.

ROSE. Read it again.

CLANCY. I didn't even read my *own* book twice.

ROSE. Maybe that's why your stones sank to the bottom. *(She crosses to the stairs.)* Goodnight, Mr. Clancy, I'll see you in the morning. *(WALSH is in between ROSE and CLANCY.)* Coming up?

CLANCY. What was that?

ROSE. They say a storm is coming up. It's the perfect time to read a book.

WALSH. I'm not coming up. I'm going to stay right here and see that he doesn't skip pages.

ROSE. *(To WALSH.)* I said come up. *(CLANCY looks at her again.)* Come up, come up, oh storm of the sea, oh brich, oh brawning, a brook on the glee. Robert Burns...I'm sure you know him.

CLANCY. I never met him...Oh I see. *(ROSE starts up the stairs.)* Do you mind if I have a beer or two? You have Heineken?

ROSE. Heineken is the only thing I drink.

(ROSE beckons with her thumb for WALSH to come up. He starts up the stairs.)

WALSH. We're gonna work tonight Rosie. We set the bait, he takes the hook and we pull together.

ROSE. *(To WALSH.)* Ooh, baby, baby...I love when you talk like that.

(CLANCY looks troubled as the lights go out.)

Scene 4

(Early dawn.
Sun is barely up. CLANCY is asleep on the sofa, the book spread across his chest, two empty Heinekens on the floor.
ARLENE comes out carrying a tray of hot coffee, a bagel and scrambled eggs. She puts it down, looks at him a moment. She takes off the woolen sweater around her shoulders and covers him with it.)

CLANCY. *(Sits up, rubs his face.)* Smells good. What time is it?

ARLENE. Six thirty.

CLANCY. Oh, am I up?

ARLENE. Well, you *look* up. I put some breakfast on the table for you.

CLANCY. *(Starts to sit up.)* You always get up this early?

ARLENE. Sometimes earlier. I'm not a good sleeper.

CLANCY. I could teach you how. You've got my number. *(He looks up at her.)* What?

ARLENE. Nothing. It just sounded a little inappropriate to me.

CLANCY. I know....but its only six thirty in the morning. *(He picks up coffee.)* You just visiting Rose or do you live with her?

ARLENE. I stay with her. For the summer.

CLANCY. I see. You *stay* with her....What's in it for you?

ARLENE. I don't understand.

CLANCY. Sure you do...What do *you* get out of it?

ARLENE. Friendship.

CLANCY. Don't you have any men friends you could stay with for the summer? *(She glares at him.)* What? Another inappropriate remark?

ARLENE. Well, most of them seem to be. She's my closest friend. I've known her for years.

CLANCY. How close does it get?

ARLENE. If you hand me your cup of coffee, I'd be glad to throw it in your face.

CLANCY. It wouldn't be the first time....This is my third set of eyebrows.

ARLENE. Why are you taunting me?

CLANCY. Just seeing how far I can go.

ARLENE. Well, you can go back to Quogue as far as I'm concerned.

(She starts to leave.)

CLANCY. I don't think so, she's up waiting to hear what I thought of the book....I also saw you looking at me while I slept....Is that why you brought me breakfast?

ARLENE. No. We're just civilized here.

CLANCY. Yeah. I heard that about East Hampton. That's why I stay in Quogue.

ARLENE. Look, I don't have time to trade petty banter with you.

I have better things to do.

CLANCY. Like what? What better things do you have to do...If I may ask.

ARLENE. I'm writing a screenplay at the moment.

CLANCY. So, you're a writer....This place is lousy with them.... Do I get to read your screenplay too?

ARLENE. Mr. Clancy, I think you woke up on the wrong side of the couch.

CLANCY. Really? I usually wake up on the floor.

ARLENE. I can see why. *(She picks up empty beer bottles.)* The gutter would be more appropriate.

CLANCY. Yeah. I know...I'm pretty seedy in the morning....I like your legs, if that's not too inappropriate.

ARLENE. Are you expecting a response to that?

CLANCY. It wasn't a crack. It's right here in the book. *(He opens the book, turns the pages, stops and reads.)* Here...Jake says to Madge...."I'm pretty seedy in the morning....I like your legs, if that's alright to say"....Written right here by the master.

ARLENE. Yes. She's a very great writer.

CLANCY. That may be so...but she didn't write this—Walsh McLaren did...By the way, there's dust on the pages.... *(He blows the dust out.)* How long has it been sitting around the house?

ARLENE. I don't know what you're talking about.

CLANCY. Well, I didn't say it was a conspiracy but something's fishy around here.....She gets me here to help her finish a book... Except this isn't hers...I've read every Walsh McLaren story ever written....He puts his mark on every page like the numbers on a treasury bill...Only I've never seen this book before....So why is she doing this?

ARLENE. I'm not sure....I only give directions.

CLANCY. Well, why don't we ask the great lady. When does she get up?

ROSE. *(Coming down the steps.)* When she smells hot coffee.... Would you like another Heineken for breakfast Mr. Clancy?

CLANCY. No thanks.....Do you always wake up in a smart suit?

ROSE. I don't really know...I think angels dress me in the morn-

ing. (ARLENE hands her a cup of coffee.) Thank you, dear...

ARLENE. Did you sleep well?

ROSE. No. Not yet....You're quite right, Clancy. It's Walsh's book. Not mine...I didn't think I'd be able to keep it a secret for long...

CLANCY. Did you know Walsh?

ROSE. Slightly. He came here for lunch once and died on the patio.

CLANCY. Sorry. *(To ARLENE.)* Did you know Walsh McLaren as well?

ARLENE. Not in person.

CLANCY. *(To ROSE.)* And how did you get this book?

ROSE. He left it on the table. In gratitude for the lunch.

CLANCY. *(To ROSE.)* And you're trying to pass it off as your own?...Any publisher over 45 would spot this in a minute.

ROSE. You're so clever...I'll bet you never spilled a drop of oil from that freighter....No, I'm not trying to pass off the book as mine... It will have Walsh's name on it and his name only...It's his name that will sell the book.

CLANCY. And why did he leave an *unfinished* book?

ROSE. Well, he didn't have time to finish it before he hit the flagstone.

CLANCY. Look, I may not wear clothes as smart as you but I'm not as dumb as you think....However he died, you're going to need proof he left it to you. His estate would need verification, otherwise you and I will have to defend ourselves in court.

ROSE. I'm the executor of his estate and the sole owner of all his copyrights.

CLANCY. He gave you that too? That must have been some lunch....and who would publish it? If the public finds out it was a ghost writer, they would stay away from it like the plague.

ROSE. What if I told you that as you and I work on these last 40 pages it will have Walsh McLaren's hand on it.

CLANCY. From the grave or do you keep it in the house?

ROSE. You lack *tact*, among other things...He left me copious notes on how the book *should* be finished...And don't you dare be disrespectful to one of America's great literary figures.

CLANCY. I was out of line. Slap me anytime you want.

ROSE. Maybe after lunch.

CLANCY. May I see the copious notes?

ROSE. I don't remember where I put them.

CLANCY. You don't know where the copious notes are that Walsh gave you regarding a dusty book that looks like it hasn't been open since I went to college.

ROSE. College? I wouldn't have thought you did...Where did you go?

CLANCY. To William and Mary.

ROSE. Did you finish?

CLANCY. Just William.

ROSE. Make up your mind. If you want to work on it with me, and we complete it, I'll give you ten percent of my royalties.

CLANCY. *(Smiles.)* I wondered why you didn't go to a better known writer...I would do this for nothing but since I got my foot in the door, I'll push it open...How about fifty percent?

ROSE. If I were you, I'd take my offer and buy yourself a garage in Quogue.

CLANCY. A new book by Walsh McLaren is worth half the beachfront in Quogue. You made your offer, I made mine.

(WALSH appears.)

WALSH. Take it, Rose. Take it. Don't slam the door on him.

ROSE. Well, you know where the door is, Mr. Clancy. Good luck on the rest of your shattered career.

WALSH. Geez!

CLANCY. *(Shrugs, smiles.)* Suits me. Do I owe you for the Heinekens?

WALSH. Where's he going?

ROSE. It didn't work out.

WALSH. In two minutes?

CLANCY. *(He gets up, to ARLENE.)* The crack about your leg still goes.

(He turns, leaves.)

WALSH. Don't let him go, for chrissakes. We don't have time to negotiate.

ROSE. I'll de damned if I let him swindle me and belittle you.

ARLENE. Belittle *me*?...Oh. Walsh must be back.

WALSH. *(To ROSE.)* Let's hear what he has to say about the book first, dammit.

ROSE. Why? I don't think he could write his way out of an open elevator. I've made up my mind!

WALSH. *(To ROSE.)* Call him. *Now!*...Or I'll never climb those steps again.

ROSE. With a gun in my ribs. Arlene, get Clancy back.

ARLENE. Is that what Walsh wants?

ROSE. Walsh is dead. It's *my* idea. Everything he says is my idea.

ARLENE. *(Rushes out.)* Mr. Clancy!

WALSH. *(To ROSE.)* Everything I say is *not* your idea. Everything I say is what you *think* I would say if I were here.

ROSE. But you're *not* here so you have nothing to say that matters.

ARLENE. *(Comes back in.)* He's coming....

ROSE. *(To WALSH.)* And don't tell me what to do.

ARLENE. Did Walsh just say something?

ROSE. I am not your translator, Arlene.

(CLANCY walks in, cigarette in his mouth.)

CLANCY. I *thought* I'd get a call back.

ROSE. Don't be cocky with me. And put that cigarette out in Quogue...Tell me what you thought of the book.

CLANCY. A little outdated but no one writes that good today... What's the title?

ROSE. "Mexican Standoff."

CLANCY. Perfect. No one's alive at the finish.

ROSE. We don't *know* what the finish is.

CLANCY. It was a suggestion.

WALSH. Not bad. He's ahead of us, Rose. We either change the title or the finish.

ROSE. Get your pad, Arlene…..Eavesdropping on nothing is pointless.

(ARLENE goes.)

CLANCY. *(To ROSE.)* So what's with you two?

ROSE. Which two?

CLANCY. You and her….Did I miss anyone?

ROSE. Arlene and I are not lovers, if that's what you think. And I don't give a damn what you think.

CLANCY. No offense…..but she jumps through hoops whenever you want her to….So I thought—you know. Gertrude Stein and Alice.

ROSE. Gertrude Stein and Alice weren't lovers…They were just in the same outfit in the first World War.

WALSH. *(To ROSE.)* Ask him about the book…time is fleeting.

ROSE. Tell me what you think the book is about.

CLANCY. Deceit. Two people who never said an honest word to each other…"Mexican Standoff."

WALSH. So far so good.

ROSE. I don't agree at all. Not being able to tell the truth is an ailment. Deceit is not telling the truth to gain advantage.

WALSH. Well, it comes to the same thing.

CLANCY. I don't see the difference.

WALSH. I think I like this kid.

ROSE. *(To WALSH.)* Then why don't *you* work with him?

CLANCY. With who?….

ARLENE. With Walsh's book, she means.

CLANCY. *(To ROSE.)* Look, you asked me to tell you what the book was about and I told you.

ROSE. Arlene, read back what you have.

ARLENE. I don't have anything.

WALSH. This is not the way to collaborate, Rose.

CLANCY. *(To ROSE.)* Anyway, you just can't take things out of context and—

ROSE. Walsh *never* wrote anything out of context—

WALSH. *(To CLANCY.)* Well, I did when I needed it.

ROSE. *(To WALSH.)* Will you let me handle this?

CLANCY. *(To ROSE.)* Do you always practice everything you're going to say?

ROSE. Yes. That's how I avoid rewriting.

CLANCY. Look, Walsh never gave the slightest hint where the book was going.

WALSH. That's called "style" kid.

CLANCY. Or maybe he just got stuck.

WALSH. I was unstuckable.

ROSE. *I cannot work like this.*

WALSH. Sorry.

CLANCY. Sorry.

ROSE. And stop repeating everything.

CLANCY. I just said it once.

ROSE. We can't all work together at the same time.

CLANCY. You mean the both of us.

ROSE. And Walsh.

CLANCY. Walsh?

ARLENE. She didn't mean Walsh. She meant you and her.

ROSE. Stay out of this Arlene.

ARLENE. I will. I swear. I'm out.

ROSE. *(To ARLENE.)* Are you taking notes?

ARLENE. I never hear where the notes should be.

ROSE. Well try harder.

CLANCY. Can we get back to the book? Don't you find it strange that this was the page that Walsh stopped on?

WALSH. Not in the least.

ROSE. Not in the least.

CLANCY. Why not?

ROSE. Because he was a writer. And when writers die, there's always a page they stop on.

CLANCY. This is confusing. Why don't we back up a few pages and go for our *own* ending?

ROSE. Which is what?

CLANCY. I don't know yet.

ROSE. Are there any other writers in Quogue who can help us?

WALSH. It's falling apart, Rose. Crumbling in front of our eyes.

ROSE. *(To WALSH.)* Well what do you expect *me* to do about it?

CLANCY. Well as I suggested, why don't we back up a few pages and go for our *own* ending?

ROSE. *(To CLANCY.)* We've gotten off to a bad beginning, Clancy. Why don't we call it a day?

WALSH. Not yet, Rose. We need him.

ROSE. I don't think we do.

CLANCY. Why do I get the feeling it's not me you're talking to?

WALSH. Don't answer that, Rose.

ROSE. I'll answer what ever I feel like....Mr. Clancy, I have something to tell you....

WALSH. Don't do it, Rose...

ARLENE. It's not a good idea, Rose.

ROSE. Will you both shut up...

CLANCY. I thought I already did.

ROSE. *(Gesturing to WALSH.)* Okay, Mr. Clancy, meet Walsh McLaren....Don't bother looking, you won't see him....But he's right here in the room with us...

WALSH. God dammit.

CLANCY. I see....Well, there's a medical name for that.

ROSE. The name for it is obsession. *My* obsession...He resides in my head and my soul. Do you know what I'm talking about?

CLANCY. Overwork?

ROSE. I have nightly conversations with a dead man. Well, we have *more* than conversations....Some nights we—

ARLENE. *Dance*....Often I hear them dancing.

WALSH. Stop it, Rose. You've gone too far.

ROSE. *(To WALSH.)* You sent for him. I didn't.

CLANCY. Actually, it was Arlene.

ARLENE. I just gave him directions.

ROSE. This was a mistake, Mr. Clancy....ever since you arrived from Quagmire....

CLANCY. *Quogue.*

ROSE. I *know* its Quogue. I was making a point.

CLANCY. And it's a very good point....we're *all* in a quagmire here...But I have an idea, Miss Steiner.

ROSE. Why don't you tell it to Mr. McLaren.

CLANCY. Well, I would but you'd think I was just humoring you.

ROSE. I don't think there's anything you could say that would humor me...I think you're unqualified to finish this book....I've let this go too far....I've revealed to you something I wouldn't even tell my own mother. *(CLANCY's head turns.)* Don't look for her. My mother died forty years ago. I would like you to leave now.

CLANCY. Wait. Please.....I believe you see him. I believe you hear him. I envy your being able to spend so much time with him.

ROSE. Fine. Why don't you stay and work out your ideas with Mr. McLaren?

WALSH. God dammit Rose, stop it. You're making a travesty of this.

ROSE. *(To WALSH.)* Why not? It's my travesty. *(To CLANCY.)* Walsh is leaving my life soon. Out of sight and out of my head. His attempt to secure my future with an annuity was a pipe dream, much as he is.

CLANCY. I didn't mean it to cause a problem between you two.

ROSE. Arlene, would you show him the door.

CLANCY. *(To ROSE.)* Would you...would you mind if I said goodbye to Mr. McLaren?

ROSE. Yes. This is not a ride at Disneyland. Show him the door, Arlene.

ARLENE. He *knows* where it is.

(She goes out to the door.)

ROSE. Good day, Clancy. And please don't tell the *New York Post* about this...They'll want pictures of the four of us... *(He starts to go.)* Come and see Arlene again....For some reason I think she doesn't mind you.

CLANCY. I'd like that....Can I take the book home and read it again? I think I understand it now.

WALSH. Say yes, Rose.

ROSE. Walsh wants me to say yes.

CLANCY. Thank you....Both of you...Goodbye. *(He goes out, stops, comes back in again.)* Mr. McLaren? I was honored more than you can ever know. *(To ROSE.)* I'm sorry. I couldn't help it.

(He leaves.)

ROSE. *(To ARLENE.)* Arlene, see that he brings the book back tomorrow.

WALSH. And what are you going to do for money now, Rose?

ROSE. I'll rent the house...Maybe I'll sell it.

WALSH. This is the only house you have.

ROSE. I'll teach literature...if I can remember it.

ARLENE. Is this because of me, Rose? Don't do it because of what I said. I know how much you love this place.

ROSE. Sometimes you have to let go of what you love.

WALSH. Tell me about it. *(He starts to go.)* We've got twelve days left, Rose...you can agree to work with him or practice waving goodbye to me.

ROSE. *(Looks at him, then turns to ARLENE.)* Arlene...Get him back.

ARLENE. *(Smiles.)* YESSS!

(She runs off.)

ROSE. My God! The girl is actually alive.

(Blackout.)

Scene 5

(A few days later. It's early in the morning. ROSE is at the typewriter, squinting and typing. She is wearing the same dress, or clothes that she did for the scene that was in here before. ARLENE enters.)

ARLENE. Oh...you're up early...Are you working on the book?
ROSE. No Arlene, I'm not.
ARLENE. Because Clancy called and said he had a few ideas.
ROSE. How few?
ARLENE. I don't know. Shall I ask him to come over?
ROSE. No. Tell him to keep working on his Heinekens.
ARLENE. I think he's pretty smart Rose.
ROSE. Well he got smart a little too late. The book is over. I just got a goodbye letter from Walsh.
ARLENE. He wrote a letter?
ROSE. I think he did and what I think he thinks is usually true. Wanna hear it?
ARLENE. Yes, of course.
ROSE. *(She reads to ARLENE.)* ...Dear Rose,

When you awake this morning, I will be gone...Gone forever.

I'm terribly sorry to leave so abruptly but it was bound to happen one day...I lied to you a few days ago...Or you lied to yourself...The reason I'm leaving is not that I'm 65...I don't know how old I am. Once you die, you become ageless...It's only the living who count the years they're gone...I left because wherever I'm going to, or always have been since we first parted, was to save your sanity.

The trouble, as we both know, is that we played this game too long...Seeing me day in and day out, sleeping in the same bed night after night, indulging in sexual pleasures that only you could think of...never really happened. It's because you had such a vivid imagination that we were both able to play out whatever you chose to create...It was oh so wonderful.

And I fear that if I don't leave now, it will eventually destroy your reason.

It's time to live your *own* life, Rose, and think of me only from that past...I'm not really here, Rose. Live your own life now, because you still have so much to offer to the world.

Do I love you as you imagined for these last five years?...I guess I must have...because in all the years I rested in my tomb, or the place that some people call heaven, I always longed for you...or perhaps that's what you wanted me to do...So I say goodbye, Rose...And looking to see that whatever love gave us in our days during life, will continue in some peaceful haven that so few of us believe in...

Live on, Rose, my sweet, my beautiful Rose.

I won't be coming back to you...ever...I suppose...This letter is my own true hand that writes in your mind.

It's complicated to make sense of this...But you're smart enough to handle it...Love, Walsh.

(She lays the letter on the table.)

ARLENE. Oh, God...That's the most wonderful letter I ever heard.

ROSE. Yes, isn't it?...The problem is...Did I write it...Or did Walsh?

(Fade out.)

ACT II

Scene 1

(Four weeks later. ARLENE stands looking out the windows. She glances at the phone, then decides to use it. She picks up and dials...)

ARLENE. *(Obviously leaving a message.)* Clancy, it's Arlene... Sorry I missed you. Yes, dinner tonight is fine... Rose told me to tell you she doesn't want to discuss the book...Better not call here...I'll call you later.

CLANCY. You don't have to.

(He is at the screen door on outside porch. She turns quickly.)

ARLENE. Oh, God...I thought it was...

CLANCY. Walsh?...Don't count me out yet...Sometimes I just look like I passed away.

(He comes in. She hangs up the phone, looks up towards the staircase.)

ARLENE. That's not funny...She's taking a nap upstairs.

CLANCY. Alone, or is the big guy taking one with her?

ARLENE. Shhh!

CLANCY. Sorry. I actually came over to tell her I did about twenty pages of Walsh's book.

ARLENE. You did? I don't know how she'll take that.

CLANCY. She'll never see it. Writing it was climbing uphill and

39

what came out was all downhill...I know when I'm licked.

ARLENE. I'm sorry you went to all the trouble.

CLANCY. No sweat...Walsh wrote in rhythms that even Mozart would envy...And his characters are so complex, I'd have to send the book through MIT first...His title was prophetic. We all ended up in a Mexican standoff.

ARLENE. Is that the book you have there?

CLANCY. This? No. This is a sequel.

ARLENE. To what?

CLANCY. To my first and only book. Rose got my juices going again...It doesn't stand up to Walsh's but it stands up to me.

ARLENE. I'd love to read it.

CLANCY. Just the title page. I'm not ready to open the show yet.

(He hands it to her. She looks at the first page.)

ARLENE. "Death on the Patio"...Is this about Rose and Walsh?

CLANCY. Yes. In a way.

ARLENE. In what way?

CLANCY. In a specific way...Of course it's them.

ARLENE. Gavin, what have you done? She'll sue you for plagiarism.

CLANCY. Why? I'd give her fifty percent of my profits.

ARLENE. She doesn't want your profits...Not if you reveal these last few years with her and Walsh. Don't expose the fantasies of a sick woman.

CLANCY. I never thought of her as sick. She refused to betray his work at the cost of a renewed lifestyle for her...It's a ghost story, Arlene, with a ghost that has more charm, dignity and compassion than any walking spirit since Hamlet's father...And a hell of a lot funnier...I don't mock her. I glorify her.

ARLENE. It's her life and Walsh's after life written by her, real or not, and whatever she heard or thought she heard is her sole property.

CLANCY. I'm trying to do for her what Walsh wanted. To give her last years some comfort...Walsh's book or my book? What difference does it make?

ARLENE. Because you can't quote conversations that no one ever heard...including Rose...And what makes you so sure you'd ever make a dime out of your book?

CLANCY. Well, I did give it a sneak look at Doubleday...They offered me more fingers than I ever counted on...But I won't take it until she approves.

ARLENE. She won't.

CLANCY. I think she will...It was Walsh's last request. Now I can fulfill it...I can't bring him back but maybe I can bring back what he wanted to leave her...

ARLENE. Who said he did? Only she heard it. And she heard only what she wanted to hear.

CLANCY. She remembered the cupboard where his book was... She took it out. Whose idea was it to get it completed and make her some money?...Maybe it was her conscience that made it Walsh's idea. Maybe she's the one who put my book in his pocket.

ARLENE. Maybe...I just want to protect her.

CLANCY. That woman protects herself. If she were in the army she would be a tank...The woman has warded off everything thrown at her...The U.S. Government questioned her loyalty...Theater critics allowed her two or three big hits, then started throwing bricks at her... She hung around with an alcoholic genius who was never faithful to her...All that and not a single living relative in the world to stand up for her...Am I right about all that?

ARLENE. Except for the single living relative.

CLANCY. She has one? *(She nods.)* Who?

ARLENE. A daughter...

CLANCY. Where is she?

ARLENE. Right here...talking to you.

CLANCY. Is this a joke?

ARLENE. Do I look like a joke?

CLANCY. When did this happen?

ARLENE. A long time ago...in New Orleans...She knew her life was no place to raise a baby and the father, my father, offered to take me off her hands...

CLANCY. Why didn't she tell anyone?

ARLENE. Because it might have scandalized all three of us... "Rose Steiner's abandoned baby" and things like that...But I wasn't. I was just out on loan...She sent me gifts every Christmas and took me to dinner every birthday...We never had a mother and daughter relationship and that was fine with me...I loved my father...and she and I were friends without obligations...She probably wouldn't have made a very good mother but she became my best friend. And I like calling her Rose instead of Mom.

CLANCY. And no one knows this?

ARLENE. No one that I know. Not even Walsh.

CLANCY. Of all people, why are you telling *me* all this?

ARLENE. To stop you from making a fool of her in your book.

CLANCY. *(Hands book to her.)* Read the book. If you don't like it, I'll burn it with the rest of my unpublished offerings.

ARLENE. And if you tell anyone what I just told you, we'll deny everything you say...And I'll sue you.

CLANCY. Despite the fact that you have a crush on me.

ARLENE. What?

CLANCY. ...Will you sue me if I put *that* in the book?

ARLENE. Probably...Can I read your book tonight?

CLANCY. We were going to dinner.

ARLENE. I can read and eat at the same time.

CLANCY. I knew there was something interesting about you... Now I see you're God damn fascinating.

ARLENE. Guess where I got it from?

CLANCY. Is it because you wanted to take care of your mother that you never married?

ARLENE. No.

CLANCY. Then why?...

ARLENE. Because Walsh was the love of her life...and even though I never met him, I was looking for someone like him.

CLANCY. Even though he wasn't always faithful to her?

ARLENE. So you give up a little sometimes.

CLANCY. Would you be satisfied with that? Someone who wasn't always faithful to you?

ARLENE. Are you proposing an unfaithful relationship to me?

CLANCY. No. I already had one...Do I remind you of Walsh?

ARLENE. No. He lived in my mother's mind...You're just—

CLANCY. What?

ARLENE. Just a guy from Quogue.

CLANCY. You don't find Quoguees attractive?

ARLENE. A little...But it'll go away in the morning.

CLANCY. What if I didn't go away in the morning?

ARLENE. Gavin, there's not a chance in the world that you and I would— *(He grabs her and kisses her fully on the lips...She doesn't return it...He pulls back.)* —get together so quickly.

CLANCY. I'm sorry. I shouldn't have done that.

ARLENE. No, I liked it...Just warn me first.

*(She smiles at him. He looks at her, surprised.
Dim out.)*

Scene 2

(A few days later. ARLENE is putting lunch on the table. It is a very sunny day.)

ARLENE. Would you like some lunch, Rose?

ROSE. I'm sick of your watery tuna salad.

ARLENE. Do you want to come down or shall I bring it up?

ROSE. If you bring it up, I'll only throw it up...Take it away. I don't want to see it.

ARLENE. *(Puts a cloth over it.)* I'll put it outside for the dog.

ROSE. What dog?

ARLENE. The one who comes around every day to eat the breakfast I made for you.

ROSE. Stop making breakfast for strange dogs. We're trying to save money...Just give him a bagel and cream cheese and send him on his way. *(ROSE slowly comes down the stairs. It's the first time we see her disheveled. A robe over a worn sleeping gown. Her hair is frizzed and unbrushed and she wears men's slippers. The sun hits her in the eyes. She puts her hand up to get it out of her eyes.)* I told you to get rid of the sun.

ARLENE. I've tried. It persists in shining.

ROSE. Except when you want to go to the beach...Why don't you close the blinds?

ARLENE. Then you say it's too gloomy in here.

ROSE. Gloom is very popular these days. *(ARLENE closes the blind, turns on some lamps.)* Go on. Run up our electric bill. You can pay it out of your salary.

ARLENE. You don't pay me a salary.

ROSE. And you can see why. *(Goes to the door to the beach, looks out.)* Have any dead writers washed up on the beach?

ARLENE. Stop it, Rose. That's not funny.

ROSE. He would think so.

ARLENE. Why don't you get dressed and we'll take a walk.

ROSE. Wearing what?...I'm selling all my clothes. I'm trying to support myself...Do I have anything you'd like...You can have it for ten percent off.

ARLENE. It's not really my style, Rose.

ROSE. No. You're much prettier than me. You can thank your father for that.

ARLENE. You always said brains before beauty.

ROSE. Of course. I was hopeful someone would believe me.

ARLENE. Let's get out of the house, Rose. You can't sit in here and mourn forever.

ROSE. I only mourn some of the time. It's the trouble with people who won't stay dead...Why don't you go see what's his name? I hear you talking to him. Francie, was it?

ARLENE. Clancy. You know it's Clancy. Stop pretending you've aged ten years in the past four weeks.

ROSE. I'm not pretending. Sometimes it's important for a woman my age to let herself fall apart. It's like a pit stop to eternity... That was good. Write it down so I can put it in my next book.

ARLENE. Are you thinking of a next book?

ROSE. I'm always thinking of one. It's better than writing one... Ask my publisher if I can sell a book I'm just thinking about.

ARLENE. Well there's another book...Gavin wrote it. I don't think you'd like it very much...It's about you and Walsh...He doesn't use your names but anyone who knows you will figure it out.

ROSE. And what do you want me to do? Sue him for libel...

ARLENE. He wants permission from you to publish the book. Doubleday offered him ten times what he made on his first book... And for your permission, he'll give you half his royalties...

ROSE. Did you read it?

ARLENE. Twice.

ROSE. Is it any good?

ARLENE. He has no right to publish it.

ROSE. That's not my question...Is it good, Arlene?...Is it prose worthy?

ARLENE. Well, he has style...Obviously following in the footprints of Walsh...I think most critics will see through it.

ROSE. Just answer my question.

ROSE. It's not bad...But reminiscent.

ROSE. Of what?

ARLENE. "Mexican Standoff."

ROSE. How are the last forty pages?

ARLENE. Well, that's the odd thing. The last forty pages are quite good.

ROSE. Dear God...

ARLENE. What is it, Rose?

ROSE. "Rest in Pieces."

ARLENE. What about it?

ROSE. Lately I've been wondering how Clancy's book, got into Walsh's bathrobe pocket...and I suddenly remembered. *(She turns and looks at ARLENE.)* ... I found it in a second hand book shop.....in the mystery section....Sometimes Walsh was in the mystery section and sometimes in the literature...I would always take it out of the mystery and put it in literature where it belonged...I saw the title "Rest in Pieces," which I didn't particularly like but it sounded like a younger Walsh...And when Walsh was out of the room, I slipped it into his robe pocket.....I put it there.

ARLENE. Let's go into town. I made an appointment with Carlotta to do something with your hair.

ROSE. No. She makes my head look like a postage stamp from Lithuania...Besides, she charges too much.

ARLENE. Then I'll pay for your hair.

ROSE. No. Walsh was fond of my hair. He said my hair always looked like it was thinking. *(She looks at door again.)* Come back, Walsh. Even as a Dover sole...I'll know it's you...Am I shocking you, Arlene?

ARLENE. No. I think if you talk about him, it will at least get your mind off thinking about him.

ROSE. Think before you say things like that, Arlene. Then they'll know you went to a proper school.

ARLENE. I'll accept your insults, Rose, if we can just get out for an hour. The fresh air will do you good again.

ROSE. He might come back. I must be here if he comes back.

ARLENE. He's not coming back, Rose. You let him go forever. You didn't want to finish his book and now you're free, don't you understand?

ROSE. Free? You think I'm free?...I'm worse off than I was before...I'm a prisoner of his absence...For the rest of my life...If only I helped finish his God damned book...I gave away the last week I could have spent with him and that's what I regret...That I cherished his words more than his presence...He was everything to me...

ARLENE. If the love is so real, why did you both drink so much?

ROSE. To keep the love real...A life cold sober can do terrible things to a love affair...After he died I was sitting right there...In that chair...And I prayed to God, despite the fact I was not a religious woman, that I could see Walsh again...To talk to, to be with, to have him touch me...And then I heard his voice, his rich, warm voice say to me as if nothing had happened..."What's for dinner, Rosie"...and I looked up, petrified at first...He was sitting right there, wearing this ratty bathrobe over some pajamas and these slippers that I bought him for Christmas...He returned from the dead...and what do you think I said to him?

ARLENE. What?

ROSE. I said, "What if I sent out for Chinese?"... "Just what I was thinking," he said...I was not going to question a dead man asking for Chinese food. So I decided to accept what was given to me...I would have welcomed him if he came in a bottle of formaldehyde...He came close to me and I reached out to touch him, but I couldn't feel his face or his hand...What I touched was his essence...But it didn't frighten me because I didn't want to frighten *him*...After all, the man might not know he was dead...So we talked all night...and we laughed...and we ate the Kung Pow with the shredded chicken and dim sum with white rice...We even had the fortune cookies. And do you know what mine said?

ARLENE. Yes. "Take what is offered to you, it may not come this way again."

ROSE. That's right.

ARLENE. The summer's almost over. Let's pack up and go back to New York...See your friends, go to your favorite restaurants...Let the world see that you're still a vibrant woman.

ROSE. I can't afford false dignity. Who would I fool? My eyes grow dimmer every day...I miss him and if he did come back, I'd have to hear his voice to know he was in the room...or smell the faint cologne he wore that cost him more than he got for a short story...He was vain you know but never conceited...There's a very delicate difference, you understand.

ARLENE. Rose, we go through this every day.

ROSE. Did I ever tell you how we met?

ARLENE. A thousand times.

ROSE. Well if it's worth telling it's worth listening to again. It was a restaurant in Hollywood. The Brown Derby. I don't know if he came over to my table or I went over to his...

ARLENE. Did I ever tell you what I did when I was nineteen?

ROSE. I shouldn't be sitting here...That's his chair...He may even be in it now...I can't see him or hear him, that's my punishment.

ARLENE. Did I ever tell you what I did when I was nineteen?

ROSE. No. Why didn't you tell me when you were nineteen? *(ARLENE walks away.)* Arlene!

ARLENE. You're so unapproachable...Not even my father could get through to you...It was so daunting to talk to you...You're not someone a daughter would want to compete with.

ROSE. I never thought that's what you wanted. You should have spoken up.

ARLENE. I guess you're right. I should have spoken up.

ROSE. *(A little hurt.)* It's never too late.

ARLENE. I'm thirty four. I needed you when I was nineteen.

ROSE. Alright. Pretend you're nineteen.

ARLENE. I don't want to pretend. I'll take my chances with saying what I feel *now*. It's bad enough that I lost all those early years with you. But when I finally get here, actually move in with my own mother, I'm shut out again...I can almost understand coming in second to Walsh...but coming in second to the *ghost* of Walsh is more than I can handle...And even though it's your voice I hear in your nightly conversations with him, I tend to take his side...You hold on to him even after his death because you miss him so much and *still* you dominate the conversations...Some nights I want to call out from upstairs, "Don't let her push you around, Walsh. She let me go when I was a child and kept you after you died"...How much control does a woman need?...Sometimes I wished *he* was the child and *I* was the one who died...At least I'd have my nights with you...I cherished all the letters you sent to me because that's all I could get from you...But it's hard to hug a letter, Rose...Especially when she doesn't sign it "Mother"...

ROSE. *(Sits quietly, not moving.)* ...I think that's the longest I ever let you speak without interrupting you...Tell me what happened when you were nineteen?

ARLENE. It's over, Mom...I'm not plagued by it anymore.

ROSE. But I will for the rest of my life...Please tell me, Arlene.

ARLENE. Alright....I was angry with my father because he didn't fight hard enough to keep a mother for me...So at nineteen I had an affair...He was 41...and married...with two children...I didn't think about what his wife felt, if she knew or what his kids felt...All I knew was that somebody loved me and I didn't have to wait for my birthday for someone to show their love...It lasted eight months before his wife left him and he spent all his time trying to get her back...which left me on the phone trying to find you in Paris or London or Rome...And then I heard from you..."Darling, Mother won the Pulitzer Prize today"...And finally you came to my college graduation...to make the commencement address and at last we were together...Well at least we were commencing...

ROSE. What have I done to you?

ARLENE. You listened to me...and that's enough...

ROSE. Not for me...How do we get on with our lives?

ARLENE. Well, you can come with me and let Carlotta do your hair. *(ROSE has trouble breathing and holds her chest.)* What is it, Rose? Are you alright?...Rose?

(WALSH appears in beach door.)

ROSE. Arlene, he's here...I can't see him...Why can't I see him? He's afraid to let me see him. He's trying to fight through but I won't let him in.

ARLENE. That's it, Mom. Fight him. Fight *yourself*... Don't bring him back. He doesn't have the power you have.

ROSE. Arlene, what can I do?...Help me...Talk to me. Please.

ARLENE. Maybe it really is over, Mom...Maybe it's the end of it...Maybe it's time to let Walsh go.

ROSE. It's so hard to do.

ARLENE. Don't stop talking to me, Mom. Don't look for him... Look at me. You gave more to the world than being a mother...I think you're a great woman, Rose.

ROSE. Walsh?

ARLENE. *(Shouts.)* LEAVE HER ALONE, WALSH...THIS IS MY TIME WITH HER, NOT YOURS...GET OUT OF HER HEAD, GOD DAMMIT. GO AWAY... *(WALSH backs away. She screams at WALSH somewhere.)* I KNOW YOU'RE DEAD, WALSH...BUT I COULD KILL YOU AGAIN...TRUST ME. I'LL GIVE YOU THREE SECONDS TO GET OUT OF HERE.

ROSE. It's alright, honey....Shh...He's gone and it's alright.

ARLENE. Are you sure? Because I could get a broom or something...I kill spiders all the time.

ROSE. Arlene, Arlene...This is our time. Yours and mine...Walsh meant no harm...He wasn't even here...I did it to myself...If you like you can publish Clancy's book...It's Walsh's gift to all of us.

ARLENE. Really? Because I think I'm in love with him. With Clancy...He's a wonderful writer, honest.

ROSE. I know...I never really gave him a chance...

ARLENE. It's alright.

ROSE. I have to be strong now. Walsh won't understand...I've never done this to him before. *(Hand to heart again.)* Something's wrong, Arlene...This is not a good time for me to leave you...Call the hospital...Pack some things for me...Anything you like...Arlene, don't worry. We'll get through this too...

(Go to dark.)

Scene 3

(Early evening. ROSE comes down the staircase wearing her best robe. Her hair is combed neatly. She crosses to the porch door that leads outside. It is open. The wind blows and invigorates her. The telephone rings inside. ROSE turns as ARLENE comes in and crosses to the phone.)

ROSE. That's alright, honey. I'll get it.

(ARLENE ignores her and crosses to the phone and answers it. She is pleased.)

ARLENE. Hi. I was wondering where you were...I miss you too.
ROSE. Is that Clancy? Say hello for me.
ARLENE. *(Impervious to her.)* Well, I'm going to need some help with my suitcases...What good news?...Alright. I'll wait.
ROSE. Wait for what, honey?

(But ARLENE doesn't respond.)

ARLENE. Love you too.

(She hangs up, starts back and smiles, and goes back upstairs.)

ROSE. *(Calls out to ARLENE.)* Is anything wrong?

(No response. WALSH enters from the opened door on the outer porch. He is wearing an elegant gray pin striped suit, expensive shoes and a flower in his lapel.)

WALSH. *(Cheerfully.)* And how are we today?
ROSE. *(Turns, looks at him.)* Well, well...Been to the St. Patrick's Day Parade?
WALSH. Couldn't make it...I see enough Saints where I live anyway.

(He goes to smell flowers in a vase.)

ROSE. Getting out some old duds for the fun of it?
WALSH. No, no, Rose me darling...I've just come from a wedding...A writer friend of mine.
ROSE. What am I doing?...You're not supposed to be here...I

don't even see you anymore...Well, I do but I'm not supposed to.

WALSH. It's alright, Rose. Arlene won't see me anyway.

ROSE. I promised her it's over. I promised myself.

WALSH. Well, nothing is written in stone...except maybe hieroglyphics...Shall I tell you about the wedding?

ROSE. She may come back in. She may hear me talking to you.

WALSH. I don't think so...My friend Charles Dickens got married...Didn't write a book today so he took a wife.

ROSE. I'm not listening.

(She turns away.)

WALSH. His poor wife died two years ago so he married her sister...A lovely wedding...Herman Melville was there...Guy de Maupassant...He came with Elizabeth Browning...She came with Jane Austen.

(ARLENE enters carrying a heavy suitcase.)

ROSE. *(Whispers to WALSH.)* Please don't talk to me, Walsh. *(To ARLENE.)* Where are you going with the suitcase, dear? *(ARLENE drops the suitcase, then turns to go back up.)* Arlene! I'm talking to you.

(ARLENE is gone.)

WALSH. They get in moods like that sometimes...Truman Capote read part of the service...He read a chapter from "In Cold Blood"...Completely self-serving and out of taste.

ROSE. What's going on here, Walsh...You didn't come to tell me about a wedding.

WALSH. Well, perhaps not...

ROSE. I was feeling so good today and now you've spoiled everything.

WALSH. ...To tell the truth, Rose, you look tired. What have you been doing today?

ROSE. Nothing...Well, actually I was adding up the sum of my life...I haven't been very well liked, you know.

WALSH. Yes, but just by people.

ROSE. Oh, shut up.

WALSH. But, Arlene and I think you're wonderful...Despite the fact that you could have been a better mother.

ROSE. We've already settled that.

WALSH. Well, we'll see...There's always a few thunderbolts after a storm...Clancy, on the other hand truly admires you.

ROSE. He does, does he?...Tell me something...Is he for real or is he just you thirty years ago?

WALSH. Well, we won't know that for another thirty years...

(CLANCY comes in from the porch.)

CLANCY. Arlene!

WALSH. The kid has good timing...

(ARLENE rushes down.)

ARLENE. You rushed out so early this morning...Why didn't you wake me?

CLANCY. I left a kiss on your lips...Did you read it yet?

ARLENE. *(Puts arms around his neck.)* Are you in love or are you just feeling good?

CLANCY. How'd your day go?

ARLENE. It's still hard...I see her everywhere I go. Anyway, what happened at the meeting?

CLANCY. Damn good news. Doubleday wants the book out for Christmas.

ARLENE. I thought you said Christmas books get lost in the crowd.

CLANCY. I was misinformed.

ROSE. There's a reason they don't see me, Walsh...What is it?

WALSH. Young love. When you're in it, you could miss the

Grand Canyon.

CLANCY. *(To ARLENE.)* I met with the head of the PR department...He said he cried when he read it...He said, knowing Rose, people might think the book was fiction.

ARLENE. I can understand that. Come on upstairs. I need help with the bags. I want to close up the house tonight.

CLANCY. Why not in the morning? Tonight is too good to waste.

ARLENE. I'll toss you for it.

CLANCY. I'd love to be tossed by you.

(They go upstairs.)

ROSE. *(To WALSH.)* What did she mean, "close up the house tonight?" What's that about?

WALSH. I'm sorry, I thought this was all clear to you.

ROSE. You're getting so vague, Walsh...I think I've outgrown you.

WALSH. Not possible, Rosie. Like two Sequoia trees we touch the sky together.

ROSE. *(Looks away.)* I can't understand why Arlene or Clancy didn't say a word to me.

WALSH. Good God...You really don't know...

ROSE. Know what?... *(It hits her.)* Are you saying—

WALSH. I'm afraid so.

ROSE. ...I'm afraid to say the word...Dead?

WALSH. Or deceased...Or gone...Passed away...Demised...What else?

ROSE. I can't catch my breath.

WALSH. Well, there's a very good reason for that...You had a heart attack, Rosie...The same as I did...The result was identical.

ROSE. Why don't I feel that I'm dead?

WALSH. You would if you were still alive...Well, that's not accurate. Give it some time.

ROSE. The most important event in my life and I missed it?

WALSH. Sometimes one never knows when it actually happens...You were one of the fortunate ones.

ROSE. What's fortunate about it?

WALSH. Well, you sort of slipped through...

ROSE. Does Arlene know?...Well, of course she would...She couldn't see me...Poor baby...Were you there when it happened?

WALSH. No. I was at my club...I was told by a friend who just passed away as well.

ROSE. Were you sad...or happy?

WALSH. A little of both...I don't mean that as unfeeling as it sounds. It's bad for you, good for me.

ROSE. Rose Steiner is dead!...How unusual for me...Exactly what time did it happen?

WALSH. Is the time important?

ROSE. Every second of life is important...Am I still in my body?...No, I couldn't be...Where is my...whatever they call it?

WALSH. The loved one...as they call it...is lying at rest in Greenrose Cemetery. You'll like it...It's as green as Ireland.

ROSE. Was anyone there? No. Never mind.

WALSH. Yes, a very large crowd...People drove up from everywhere.

ROSE. Yes! What a thing for me to miss.

WALSH. Not really. You had the best seat in the house...

ROSE. And this house...Is Arlene selling it?

WALSH. From what I understand, they're just closing it for the winter. They'll be back next year...They think it's the ideal spot to write...

ROSE. And what about my furniture and my books and my clothes?

WALSH. Do you really care?

ROSE. Why does everyone have to give up everything after they die?

WALSH. Well, the galaxy is an enormous creation, but there's never enough closet space—

ROSE. *(At same time.)* —Closet space. And I suppose you and I will be together for eons and eons...

WALSH. Well, maybe just one eon.

ROSE. Still have your bags packed in the hallway, Walsh?..And of course, no more writing. *(WALSH shrugs his shoulders.)* ...I don't really mind laying down my pen, I didn't have that much left to say anyway...What we want to keep are the things we love most...The flowers we planted, the houses we built, the friends we made and the children we raised...or almost raised...I always thought when I died, I'd have the Philharmonic Orchestra there.... *(He shrugs patiently.)* No Maria Callas?

WALSH. Booked for the next three years...

ROSE. The body goes but the vanity lingers on...Can I see what I look like dead? *(He points to a mirror, she turns.)* Oh, shit!...Oh, God, I'm sorry. Is it alright to say that when you pass on?

WALSH. Millions have said it before you.

ROSE. Let me look again. *(She turns to the mirror.)* ...Actually... it's not bad...That dry skin you have as you age isn't there anymore.

WALSH. If they had a chain of stores they could make a fortune...Let's go, Rose.

ROSE. So what now?

WALSH. The tunnel is next.

ROSE. A tunnel?

WALSH. We all go through a tunnel that leads to a light at the end.

ROSE. Oh, don't make it sound like a Greet Garson movie... What tunnel? I don't like tunnels. They frighten me...Where is it?

WALSH. I can't describe it accurately but it looks very much like the Lincoln Tunnel.

ROSE. Are you telling me that I'll come out in New Jersey?

WALSH. Just take it as it comes, Rose.

(CLANCY and ARLENE come out carrying a few more suitcases.)

ARLENE. And did they settle on the title?

CLANCY. Just what I asked for "Rose and Walsh."

ARLENE. Thank you. *(She kisses his cheek.)* Gavin, could you give me five minutes alone in the house? There's something I have to do.

CLANCY. Fine...I want to take some of your mother's plants with us. Otherwise they'll freeze.

ROSE. Oh God, he'll water them with Heineken.

(CLANCY leaves.
ARLENE pours some wine from a decanter. She crosses to a place away from ROSE, sips her wine.)

ROSE. And what about Arlene? Was I able to say goodbye to her?

WALSH. That you did, Rose.

ROSE. We lost all those years and now I've lost her forever.

WALSH. No. She'll remember you even better than it was.

ARLENE. Rose...Mother...No. Mom...This drink is to you...I love you.

ROSE. And I love you too, Angel.

WALSH. *(To ROSE.)* Shhh. This isn't a conversation, Rose. This is between Arlene and herself.

ROSE. Oh. Of course.

ARLENE. I said some pretty harsh things to you when we had that long talk...I still mean them, not because I'm still angry...but I thought they would be said...And you let me...So here's to you.

(She sips some wine.)

ROSE. *(To ARLENE.)* There's a better bottle in the cellar.

WALSH. That's not the point, Rose.

ROSE. Oh.

ARLENE. It may be too late to get the record straight...But I'm proud and elated that Rose Steiner was my mother...Who wouldn't be? Please don't be angry or feel guilty when I said I missed you as a child...I'm supposed to miss you...If I didn't, what kind of a daughter would I have been? And I understand now how difficult a life it is to be judged all the time...to have to live up to expectations...If this gets too syrupy, just speak up.

ROSE. It's not syrupy at all...It's exactly what I would— *(WALSH shakes his head at her.)* Sorry, dear...I'm not used to playing this part.

ARLENE. ...You're a loving woman...I've seen that with you and Walsh...And if I didn't get all the years with you, I got the best of them...I know you had a very tough childhood...and growing up like that deprived you of a softness...that you thought it was a weakness... it's not, Mom...I see that now...Walsh wasn't always an easy man to spend your life with...

ROSE. There. You see?

ARLENE. But he saw through your toughness...He saw the loving part of you...

WALSH. She's telling you she understands, Rose...She's giving you a higher grade than you ever got before.

ARLENE. So here's to you again, Mom... *(She sips some more wine.)* There's one thing I'm sure of...That heaven will embrace you with all its love...And you'll be happy forever...

ROSE. Well, you have to go through the Lincoln Tunnel first...

WALSH. I said it looks like the Lincoln Tunnel...

ARLENE. I could talk to you like this for hours...but the glass is empty...

ROSE. Some other time then...

CLANCY. *(Comes in quickly.)* Can we go, honey. The traffic's getting heavy and I don't want to get stuck in the tunnel.

ARLENE. Goodbye, Mom. Goodbye, Walsh...Give her a kiss for me...I may call on you from time to time...

(She runs out, turning the lights off. Just one light above stays on, shining down on ROSE and WALSH.)

ROSE. *(Looks up.)* That light never turns off.
WALSH. Come on, Rose.

ROSE. I always felt so safe in this house.

WALSH. It's not your house anymore...Come on. Give me your hand...

(He stretches his hand out to her.)

ROSE. I...I'm afraid.

WALSH. Of the cold hand of death?...I wouldn't do that to you, Rose...Just place it in mine.

(Slowly she reaches out to him and he takes her hand in his.)

ROSE. I feel it...I feel it, Walsh...It's so good to feel you again... It's so warm and comforting...

WALSH. I told you...Now blow the light out.

(She looks above at the one light on and blows...the light goes out.)

CURTAIN

Neil Simon began his writing career in television and established himself as our leading writer of comedy by creating a succession of Broadway hits beginning with *Come Blow Your Horn*. During the 1966-67 season, *Barefoot in the Park, The Odd Couple, Sweet Charity* and *The Star Spangled Girl* (stock rights only) were all running simultaneously; in the 1970-71 season, Broadway theatergoers had their choice of *Plaza Suite, Last of the Red Hot Lovers* and *Promises. Promises*.

Next carne *Little Me, The Gingerbread Lady, The Prisoner of Second Avenue, The Sunshine Boys, The Good Doctor, God's Favorite, They're Playing Our Song, I Ought to Be in Pictures, Fools,* a revival of *Little Me, Brighton Beach Memoirs, Biloxi Blues* (Tony Award) a new version of *The Odd Couple* starring Sally Struthers and Rita Moreno as the title duo, *Broadway Bound, Rumors, Lost in Yonkers* (Tony Award and Pulitzer Prize), *Jake's Women* and *London Suite*.

Mr. Simon has also written for the screen: the adaptations of *Barefoot in the Park, The Odd Couple, Plaza Suite, The Last of the Red Hot Lovers, The Prisoner of Second Avenue, The Sunshine Boys, California Suite, I Ought To Be In Pictures, Chapter Two, Brighton Beach Memoirs, Biloxi Blues,* the TV motion picture of *Broadway Bound* and *Lost in Yonkers*. Other screenplays he has written include *After the Fox, The Out-of-Towners, The Heartbreak Kid, Murder by Death, The Goodbye Girl, The Cheap Detective, Seems Like Old Times, Only When I Laugh, Max Dugan Returns* and *The Marrying Man*.

SKIN DEEP
Jon Lonoff

Comedy / 2m, 2f / Interior Unit Set

In *Skin Deep*, a large, lovable, lonely-heart, named Maureen Mulligan, gives romance one last shot on a blind-date with sweet awkward Joseph Spinelli; she's learned to pepper her speech with jokes to hide insecurities about her weight and appearance, while he's almost dangerously forthright, saying everything that comes to his mind. They both know they're perfect for each other, and in time they come to admit it.

They were set up on the date by Maureen's sister Sheila and her husband Squire, who are having problems of their own: Sheila undergoes a non-stop series of cosmetic surgeries to hang onto the attractive and much-desired Squire, who may or may not have long ago held designs on Maureen, who introduced him to Sheila. With Maureen particularly vulnerable to both hurting and being hurt, the time is ripe for all these unspoken issues to bubble to the surface.

"Warm-hearted comedy … the laughter was literally show-stopping. A winning play, with enough good-humored laughs and sentiment to keep you smiling from beginning to end."
– *TalkinBroadway.com*

"It's a little Paddy Chayefsky, a lot Neil Simon and a quick-witted, intelligent voyage into the not-so-tranquil seas of middle-aged love and dating. The dialogue is crackling and hilarious; the plot simple but well-turned; the characters endearing and quirky; and lurking beneath the merriment is so much heartache that you'll stand up and cheer when the unlikely couple makes it to the inevitable final clinch."
– *NYTheatreWorld.Com*

BLUE YONDER
Kate Aspengren

Dramatic Comedy / Monolgues and scenes
12f (can be performed with as few as 4 with doubling) / Unit Set

A familiar adage states, "Men may work from sun to sun, but women's work is never done." In Blue Yonder, the audience meets twelve mesmerizing and eccentric women including a flight instructor, a firefighter, a stuntwoman, a woman who donates body parts, an employment counselor, a professional softball player, a surgical nurse professional baseball player, and a daredevil who plays with dynamite among others. Through the monologues, each woman examines her life's work and explores the career that she has found. Or that has found her.

THE OFFICE PLAYS
Two full length plays by Adam Bock

THE RECEPTIONIST
Comedy / 2m, 2f / Interior

At the start of a typical day in the Northeast Office, Beverly deals effortlessly with ringing phones and her colleague's romantic troubles. But the appearance of a charming rep from the Central Office disrupts the friendly routine. And as the true nature of the company's business becomes apparent, The Receptionist raises disquieting, provocative questions about the consequences of complicity with evil.

"...Mr. Bock's poisoned Post-it note of a play."
– *New York Times*

"Bock's intense initial focus on the routine goes to the heart of *The Receptionist's* pointed, painfully timely allegory... elliptical, provocative play..."
– *Time Out New York*

THE THUGS
Comedy / 2m, 6f / Interior

The Obie Award winning dark comedy about work, thunder and the mysterious things that are happening on the 9th floor of a big law firm. When a group of temps try to discover the secrets that lurk in the hidden crevices of their workplace, they realize they would rather believe in gossip and rumors than face dangerous realities.

"Bock starts you off giggling, but leaves you with a chill."
– *Time Out New York*

"... a delightfully paranoid little nightmare that is both more chillingly realistic and pointedly absurd than anything John Grisham ever dreamed up."
– *New York Times*

ANON
Kate Robin

Drama / 2m, 12f / Area

Anon. follows two couples as they cope with sexual addiction. Trip and Allison are young and healthy, but he's more interested in his abnormally large porn collection than in her. While they begin to work through both of their own sexual and relationship hang-ups, Trip's parents are stuck in the roles they've been carving out for years in their dysfunctional marriage. In between scenes with these four characters, 10 different women, members of a support group for those involved with individuals with sex addiction issues, tell their stories in monologues that are alternately funny and harrowing..

In addition to Anon., Robin's play What They Have was also commissioned by South Coast Repertory. Her plays have also been developed at Manhattan Theater Club, Playwrights Horizons, New York Theatre Workshop, The Eugene O'Neill Theater Center's National Playwrights Conference, JAW/West at Portland Center Stage and Ensemble Studio Theatre. Television and film credits include "Six Feet Under" (writer/supervising producer) and "Coming Soon." Robin received the 2003 Princess Grace Statuette for playwriting and is an alumna of New Dramatists.

TREASURE ISLAND
Ken Ludwig

All Groups / Adventure / 10m, 1f (doubling) / Areas
Based on the masterful adventure novel by Robert Louis Stevenson, *Treasure Island* is a stunning yarn of piracy on the tropical seas. It begins at an inn on the Devon coast of England in 1775 and quickly becomes an unforgettable tale of treachery and mayhem featuring a host of legendary swashbucklers including the dangerous Billy Bones (played unforgettably in the movies by Lionel Barrymore), the sinister two-timing Israel Hands, the brassy woman pirate Anne Bonney, and the hideous form of evil incarnate, Blind Pew. At the center of it all are Jim Hawkins, a 14-year-old boy who longs for adventure, and the infamous Long John Silver, who is a complex study of good and evil, perhaps the most famous hero-villain of all time. Silver is an unscrupulous buccaneer-rogue whose greedy quest for gold, coupled with his affection for Jim, cannot help but win the heart of every soul who has ever longed for romance, treasure and adventure.